GREEK LEGENDS

CLAIRE MORGAN

Badger Publishing Limited
Oldmedow Road,
Hardwick Industrial Estate,
King's Lynn PE30 4JJ
Telephone: 01438 791037

www.badgerlearning.co.uk

2 4 6 8 10 9 7 5 3 1

Greek Myths and Legends ISBN 978-1-78464-113-9

Text © Claire Morgan 2015
Complete work © Badger Publishing Limited 2015

All rights reserved. No part of this publication may be reproduced, stored in any form or by any means mechanical, electronic, recording or otherwise without the prior permission of the publisher.

The right of Claire Morgan to be identified as author of this work has been asserted by her in accordance with the Copyright, Designs and Patents Act 1988.

Publisher: Susan Ross
Senior Editor: Danny Pearson
Publishing Assistant: Claire Morgan
Designer: Fiona Grant
Series Consultant: Dee Reid

Photos: Cover Image: Harald Sund/Getty Images
Page 5: © DP RF/Alamy
Page 7: NASA images
Page 8: NASA images
Page 9: NASA images
Page 10: © Aflo Co., Ltd./Alamy
Page 11: Encyclopaedia Britannica/UIG/REX
Page 12: Photoservice ElectaUIG/REX
Page 13: © AF archive/Alamy
Page 15: © Ivy Close Images/Alamy
Page 16: Dorling Kindersley/Getty Images
Page 17: © Peter Horree/Alamy
Page 18: © Mary Evans Picture Library/Alamy
Page 19: Juliet Breese
Page 20: © AF archive/Alamy
Page 21: © Ivy Close Images/Alamy
Page 22: © Ivy Close Images/Alamy
Page 23: © Ivy Close Images/Alamy
Page 24: Juliet Breese
Page 25: © AF archive/Alamy, © Oliver Burston/Alamy
Page 26: © Universal Images Group Limited/Alamy
Page 27: Juliet Breese
Page 28: © Peter Horree/Alamy, © Mopic/Alamy
Page 29: © Hugh Threlfall/Alamy, © Mediablitzimages / Alamy
Page 30: © Tommy (Louth)/Alamy, © filmfoto-04edit-tech/Alamy

Attempts to contact all copyright holders have been made.
If any omitted would care to contact Badger Learning, we will be happy to make appropriate arrangements.

For Karen and Steve - tzatziki!

GREEK Myths and LEGENDS

Contents

1. Origins   5
2. Gods and goddesses   13
3. Heroes and adventures   19
4. Monsters   24
5. The Underworld   27
6. Today   29

Questions   31

Index   32

Badger LEARNING

Vocabulary

arachnids
astronomers
constellation
descendants

invincible
mythology
universe
virtuous

1. ORIGINS

Myths and legends are stories based partly on real life and partly on religious beliefs. They were very important to the Ancient Greeks thousands of years ago.

Greek myths explore important subjects such as love, power, suffering and death. They were also used by the Greeks to explain such things as:

- how the universe began
- why the planets and stars look the way they do
- elements of the natural world, such as the weather

The beginnings of the universe

The Ancient Greeks believed that before anything else existed, there was a god called Chaos. In the myths, Chaos creates three other gods, who in turn create many other gods after them.

Each god is in charge of a different part of the world:

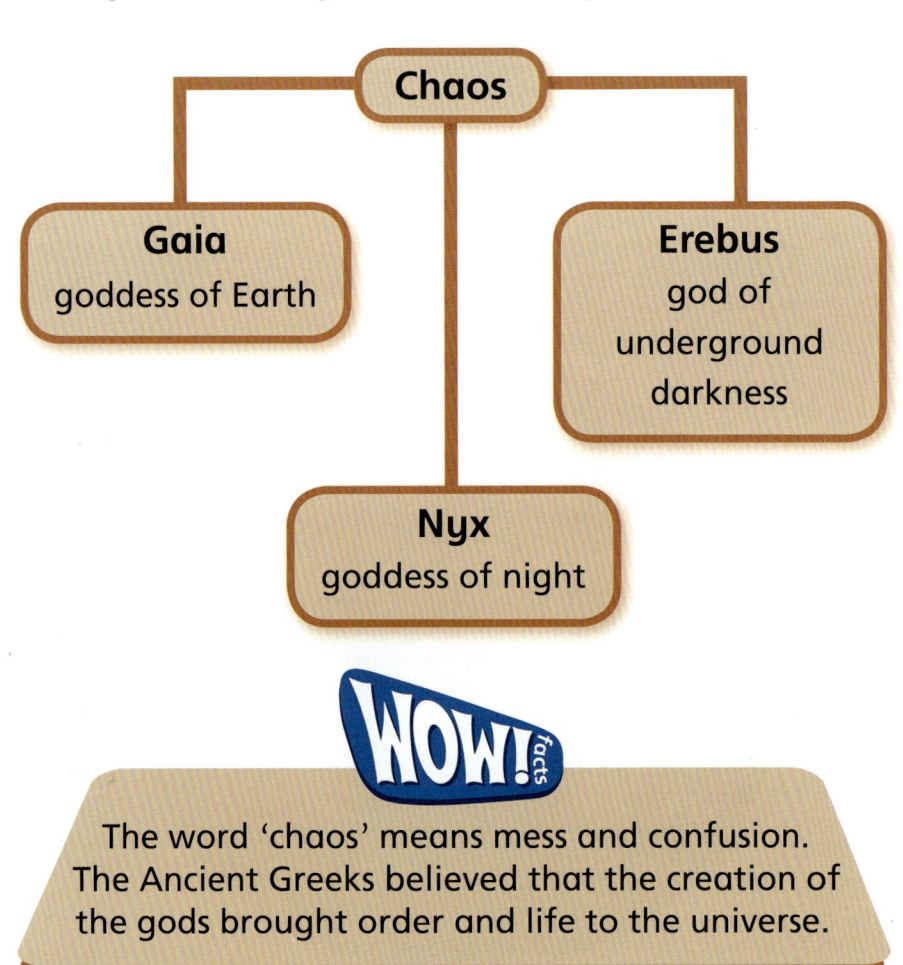

```
                    Chaos
          ┌───────────┼───────────┐
        Gaia                    Erebus
   goddess of Earth            god of
                             underground
                               darkness
                    │
                   Nyx
              goddess of night
```

WOW! facts

The word 'chaos' means mess and confusion. The Ancient Greeks believed that the creation of the gods brought order and life to the universe.

The planets

Greek astronomers explained the patterns of the stars and the planets through their stories about the gods.

The Ancient Romans copied the Greek stories of gods and goddesses but gave them their own names, which we still use today.

Hermes (Roman god Mercury)

Hermes is the messenger of the gods. He is known for being fast and the planet is probably named after him because it moves so quickly across the sky.

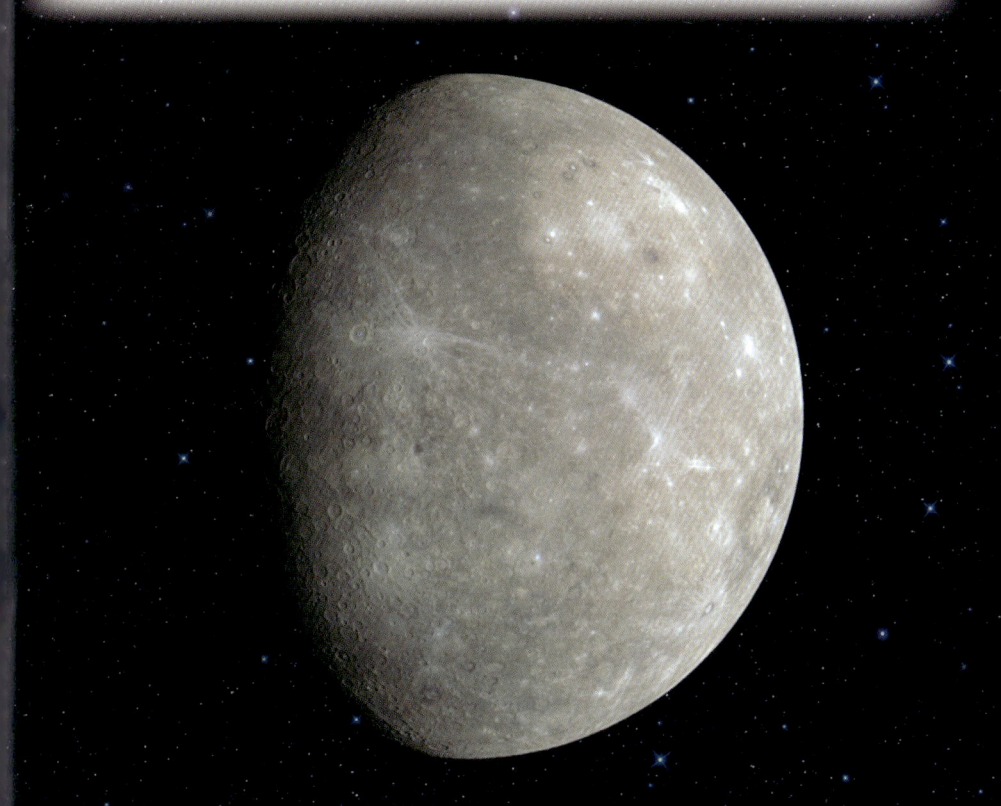

Aphrodite (Roman goddess **Venus**)
Aphrodite is the goddess of love and beauty. The planet is probably named after her because it is the brightest of the planets we can see.

Zeus (Roman god **Jupiter**)
This is the largest planet in our solar system, so that could be why it is named after Zeus, the king of the gods.

Ares (Roman god **Mars**)
This planet is blood red in colour, so it makes sense that it is named after Ares, the god of war.

WOW! facts

The word 'planet' comes from the Greek word for 'wanderer' because astronomers noticed that they moved across the sky.

The stars

Orion is a constellation of stars that takes its name from Greek mythology.

The Greek myth about Orion says that he is a hunter who is accidentally killed by his hunting partner, the goddess Artemis. She is so upset about what she has done that she puts his image among the stars in the sky.

The natural world

The Greeks used myths to explain natural events such as:

- Thunder and lightning – Zeus is king of the gods but he is also god of the weather. When he becomes angry, he throws lightning bolts as weapons. He also controls thunder, snow and hail.

- Earthquakes and sea storms – Poseidon is the god of the sea. He is known for his violent rages where he stirs up the sea with his trident. He also causes great earthquakes.

- Day and night – Apollo is the god of light. He is said to ride his chariot across the sky every day, bringing with him sunrise and sunset.

WOW! facts

In one myth, Arachne is a very skilled weaver. She boasts she is better than the goddess Athena so Athena turns her into a spider. That's why we call spiders 'arachnids'.

2. GODS AND GODDESSES

The most famous gods and goddesses from Greek mythology are the 12 gods of Olympus. They are all descendants of Gaia and rule from the highest mountain in Greece, known as Mount Olympus.

God/Goddess	Relation	God/Goddess of
Zeus	king of the gods	the weather
Hera	wife of Zeus	marriage/family
Poseidon	brother of Zeus	the sea
Hestia	sister of Zeus	home
Demeter	sister of Zeus	nature
Ares	son of Zeus and Hera	war
Hephaestus	son of Zeus and Hera	fire
Hermes	son of Zeus	messenger of the gods
Athena	daughter of Zeus	war and wisdom
Artemis	daughter of Zeus	the hunt
Apollo	son of Zeus	light/music/poetry
Aphrodite	daughter of Uranus	love

Zeus

Zeus and his brothers and sisters are children of Cronus, who is part of a group of giant gods called the Titans.

In the myths, Zeus comes to power when he leads a battle against the Titans, using his special power over thunder and lightning.

Zeus and his brothers, Poseidon and Hades, then split the world into parts so they can each rule a bit.

Zeus gets the best part, becoming lord of the sky, Mount Olympus and all the other gods.

Poseidon is made lord of the sea. He creates wild waves and storms with his magic trident, and rides a chariot pulled by seahorses.

Sailors would pray to Poseidon before a voyage, hoping that he wouldn't drown them at sea.

WOW! facts

Poseidon became known as 'Earth-Shaker' because of his powerful earthquakes.

Hades

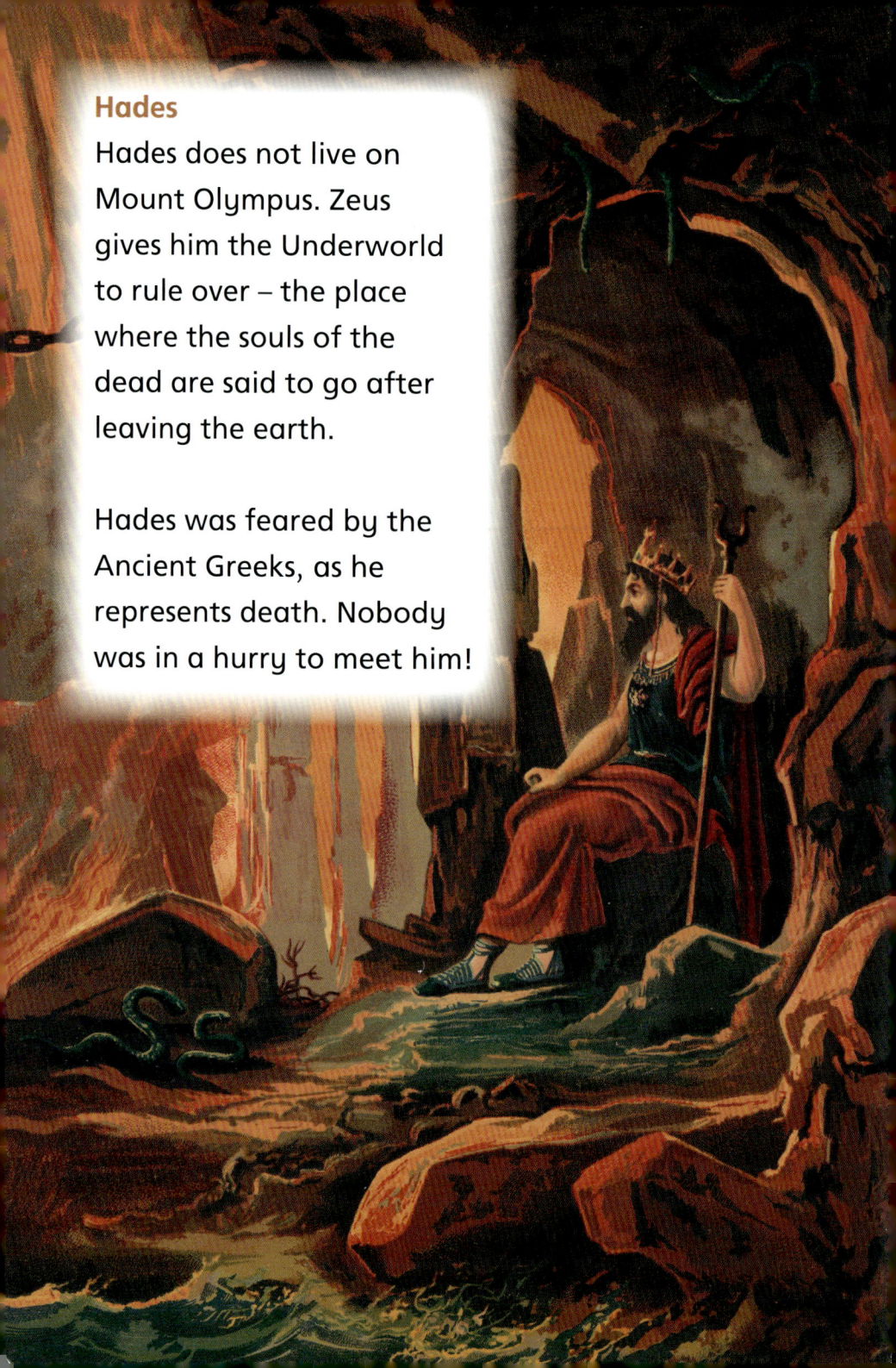

Hades does not live on Mount Olympus. Zeus gives him the Underworld to rule over – the place where the souls of the dead are said to go after leaving the earth.

Hades was feared by the Ancient Greeks, as he represents death. Nobody was in a hurry to meet him!

3. HEROES AND ADVENTURES

There are many legends about famous Greek heroes. Here are just three:

Achilles

Who he is:

The son of a human man and the sea nymph Thetis.

His story:

Thetis tries to make Achilles invincible by dipping him into the magic river Styx when he is a baby, but she has to hold him by the heel, so one spot is left unprotected.

Achilles grows to be a great fighter, but in the battle of Troy, an arrow pierces his one weak spot – his heel – and he is killed.

Heracles

Who he is:
The son of Zeus and a human queen.

His story:
Heracles is a half-god. He is known for his strength and skill as a fighter. He has to do 12 'labours' including fighting scary beasts such as a nine-headed serpent, an invincible lion and man-eating horses.

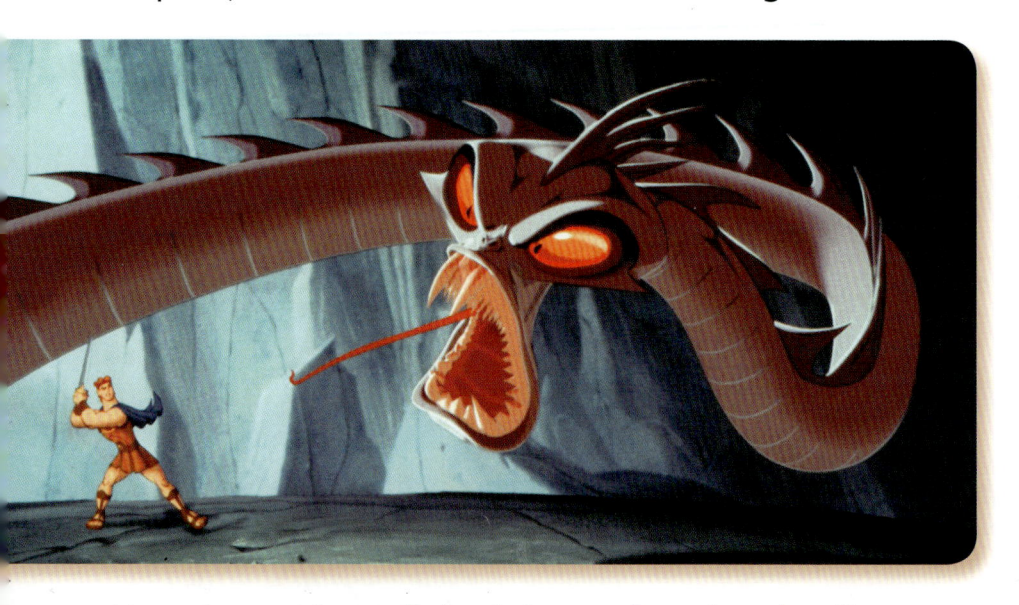

Heracles survives all the labours, but then he dies when his wife is tricked into poisoning him.

The Roman name for Heracles is Hercules.

Odysseus

Who he is:
Human king of Ithaca.

His story:
Odysseus's ship is blown off course on the way home from the Trojan war. It takes him ten years to finally make it back home, and he meets many dangers along the way:

- Sirens – creatures that use their beautiful voices to cause shipwrecks on the rocks. Odysseus gets his crew to plug their own ears and to tie him to the mast of the ship, so he can hear their song as they sail past safely.

- Cyclops – a one-eyed giant who traps Odysseus and his crew in a cave to eat them. They have to blind him and sneak past him to escape.

WOW! facts

Poseidon is very angry when the Cyclops is blinded, because the Cyclops is his son. After that, he uses his powers to keep Odysseus lost at sea.

- The Lotus-Eaters – a tribe addicted to eating a strange plant that makes you forgetful. Crew members have to be dragged back to the ship and chained to their rowing benches to escape.

- Circe – a witch who turns Odysseus's crew into pigs.

4. MONSTERS

Greek mythology is filled with terrifying monsters.

Some of them are a mixture of different animals all in one body, such as the chimera.

The chimera has:
- the head of a lion
- the tail of a serpent
- the middle of a goat

It also breathes fire!

The Hydra is a nine-headed serpent with poisonous blood and breath. When Heracles faces it, he finds that if he cuts off one of its heads, two more grow back in its place.

Charybdis is a daughter of Poseidon and takes the form of a huge whirlpool. She sucks in lots of water and throws it back up again, destroying any ships around.

Medusa is a gorgon - an ugly beast with wings, claws and snakes for hair. Legend says if you look directly at a gorgon she will turn you to stone.

Medusa is killed by the hero Perseus. He gets close to her by looking at her reflection in his shield. Then he cuts off her head!

5. THE UNDERWORLD

Hades is the god of the Underworld, which myths say is the place a person's soul goes after they die.

The river Styx surrounds the Underworld. Souls of the dead have to cross it on a boat.

A large three-headed dog, called Cerberus, guards the Underworld, making sure that no souls can escape back to the land of the living.

There are different levels within the Underworld:

Elysium is reserved for heroic and virtuous people. It is a happy place where souls can be at peace.

Tartarus is the deepest part of the Underworld where the souls of sinners are sent to be punished.

Punishments include rolling a heavy boulder up a hill, and just as it gets to the top, it rolls back down and you have to start again.

6. TODAY

Some of the names from Greek myths live on today. Some companies use those names for their products:

- The sports brand Nike is named after the Greek goddess of victory.

- Ambrosia custard – ambrosia was known as the sweet, magical food of the gods.

- Venus beauty products – Venus is the Roman name for the beautiful goddess Aphrodite.

- Atlas (book of maps) – Atlas is a Titan who Zeus punishes by making him carry the world on his shoulders.

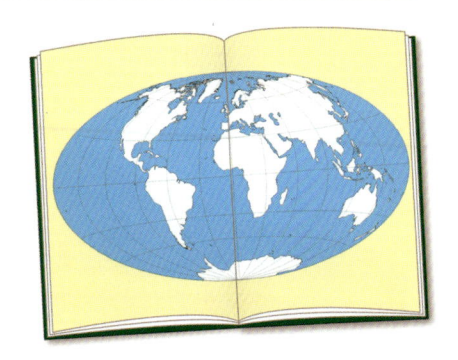

- Apollo entertainment theatres – Apollo is the god of music and poetry.

- Pegasus airlines – Pegasus is a mythical horse that can fly.

Questions

Who was the very first Greek god? *(page 6)*

Which Greek god is the planet Jupiter named after? *(page 8)*

What is Apollo the god of? *(page 14)*

Name two Greek heroes. *(pages 19-21)*

What is a chimera? *(page 24)*

Who rules the Underworld? *(pages 18 and 27)*

INDEX

Achilles 19
Ambrosia 29
Ancient Greeks 5, 6
Ancient Romans 7
Aphrodite 8, 14, 30
Apollo 12, 14, 30, 31
Arachne 12
Ares 9, 14
Atlas 30
Cerberus 27
Charybdis 25
chimera 24, 31
Circe 23
Cyclops 22
Elysium 28
Hades 16, 18, 27
Heracles 20, 25
Hermes 7, 14
Lotus-Eaters 23
Medusa 26
myths 5, 6, 11, 15, 29
Nike 29
Odysseus 21, 22, 23
Olympus 13, 16, 18
Orion 10
Pegasus 30
Perseus 26
Poseidon 11, 14, 16, 17, 22, 25
river Styx 19, 27
Sirens 21

Titans 15
Underworld 18, 27, 28, 31
Venus 8, 30
Zeus 8, 11, 14, 15, 16, 18, 20, 30